WATERMARK

Also by Jeff Hardin

A Clearing Space in the Middle of Being

No Other Kind of World

Small Revolution

Restoring the Narrative

Notes for a Praise Book

Fall Sanctuary

WATERMARK

poems

Jeff Hardin

LAKE DALLAS, TEXAS

FIRST EDITION

Requests for permission to reprint or reuse
material from this work should be sent to:

Permissions
Madville Publishing
PO Box 358
Lake Dallas, TX 75065

Cover Design: Jacqueline Davis
Cover Photo: "So Many Ways" by Donna Doyle
Author Photo: A. J. Holmes

ISBN: 978-1-948692-80-9 Paper, 978-1-948692-81-6 ebook
Library of Congress Control Number: 2021941071

for Starla, my soulmate

Contents

Phrases severe and perfect rise before me.

—Jane Hirshfield

Behind

Back behind the words
another story
is being told—

a context other
than one I
would impose.

May I dim
in some new light's
narrative

and—holding a page—
glimpse
a watermark,

as if
a whispered prayer

I so easily might have
lived without.

In the Biting Wind and Half-Dark

You
   wake to apples on the doorstep,
     as Cezanne did,

    and while it's true you're moved
      by much you see,
        you have no painter's eye

   to trace the cloudbank's swirl of plumlight. You

must
   —you can't say why—
      go out each morning,

    even in the biting wind
      and damp-grass half-dark,
        and trek along the back-fence

   edges of your life, to feel, in your bones, that

change
   from dark to light.
      What else to call it

    but a daily preparation
      for when the body turns
        to spirit, breath

   telling itself ahead of you only to fall away.

Your
   hands grow numb
      and never held much anyway

    other than the upturned, empty look of them,
      the creases and folds,
        nicks and cuts.

How perfect, you think, a poet comparing

life

     to an instance of dew,
            even if saying nothing

          of the light inside each droplet
               bound up into the only sense
                    tense makes—*now*

offered up into *always*, light offered up into more of itself.

Giving Time Back to Itself

I
> doubt so much
>> I see and hear

>> I have to steal from sleep
>>> to sort out what is true.
>>>> I find I cannot sleep

> unless I find I am awake, unless I

give
> time back to itself,
>> asking nothing more.

>> I rarely can, though,
>>> with my elegiac heart
>>>> and my lack of trust,

> my need to wring the darkness out of

myself,
> to dream of only light
>> inside of light,

>> myself inside the inside
>>> that is always growing deeper,
>>>> even as the light is growing

> wider, sweeter, farther, inexhaustible

unto
> the outer reachings of itself.
>> *Where I begin, where I leave off—*

>> I say the words' symmetry:
>>> I say their refrain,
>>>> and, like the child I am,

close my eyes and listen to my heartbeat's

prayer,
        systole and diastole,
                gather and rush.

          And when I no longer hear it
              or care that it is there,
                    I listen to my own listening

listening out past what the mind can believe.

Behind the Story Being Told

A
        quick glance down
                through hackberries

                reveals between
                        the ampersands of limbs
                                and cross-hatched, indecisive trunks

        a green I'd easily miss if not for how its

presence
        seems ordained,
                a template back behind

                the world that I can see or know.
                The same is true in conversation:
                        the words—misshapen, tangled—

        and then a sun-struck wordlessness beyond.

I
        think I hear some days
                the intercessions

                made on our behalf,
                        as numerous as dandelion stems
                                the earth itself cannot keep

        track of, seed heads given to the wind's uplifting. What

can
        each of us do
                but listen,

                allow the other's voice—naïve,
                        defenseless—a space
                                so that behind the story

being told of helping turtles cross the road, one can

feel

   even ditch grass brush along
                  one of the side-turned faces

            bound for wherever turtles go,
                  aloof on four tentative legs
                        on an earth so plentiful

   it only makes sense to trust what's out ahead.

Far From Everything

How
>>even the word "apricot"
>>>>can turn the day's course

>>>and stun the heart
>>>>is reason enough
>>>>>to search this stack of books

>>to find one word this headlong century needs.

Quiet
>>>distends memory and light-along-the-neighbor's-roof,
>>>>though who forgets

>>>>those scattered men in diners,
>>>>>hid out from their lives,
>>>>>>sparrow faces

>>>twittering behind menus while the cashier files her nails?

Must
>>be time to count the years again,
>>>>to walk beneath the squirrel nests,

>>>>one for every few trees,
>>>>>and to say aloud,
>>>>>>"I am at home here,

>>far from everything I ever wanted."

I

>>want to humble myself, whatever that means,
>>>>and keep it to myself, if possible,

>>>>me some tangible thing on the earth,
>>>>>me some theorem
>>>>>>time works out,

proving the proof of itself. I want to

be

    unknown like some hermit,
            born again each day,

        discovered some decades hence,
          bones a tidy heap,
              the roof caved in,

the sky and meadow all there ever was to say.

From There to Here

Peace
       descends like a dove,
              we're told,

           but I felt it in the air turned cool,
              in roadside leaves
                   I raced ahead to pick up then inspect

as Mother and I walked from out of the bottomlands.

I
       knew a bad thing
              had happened,

           her boyfriend putting us out,
              driving off slinging rocks and dust,
                how she bent down

to tell me words she had no use for but thought might

leave
       us in a better place.
              How long it took

           to walk back into town
              I don't remember,
                or how far it was

from there to here, this soul I've now become, a man

with
       ideas likewise left behind
              by most. *The Holy Spirit*

           walked with us, I want to say,
              and hear the sneers, the jeers,
                the curses, the door slammed.

I remember the words of Jesus: "My peace I give unto
you,"
        and then remember
                how the boy I was, still am,

           sauntered along unscathed
                down an unpaved road
                    on a late fall day,

stem-spinning leaves to see their every side turned gold.

Perfect Silence

How
        can it be my own existence
                is both a gift to enjoy,

            to inhabit fully,
                but also a burden
                    to cast aside?

        I think of old men on town-square benches, aubades

soon
        silenced by morning traffic,
                their stories once ablaze—

            skillful and sinewy, even
                profound, centered,
                    all the twists and threads,

        the once important details building to something vital—now

unaccountable,
        squandered, estranged and without purpose.
                Still, they come each day,

            take up residence.
                They while the time away.
                A kind of revenge?

        Or an acceptance of fate's decisive theme?

I
        doubt I've hid it well,
                this elegy

            for how I've come to naught
                though once I strove
                    to touch mystery upon its face,

wrenched and heaved and tore at the veil and yet

became
        as one who never tried,
                never swore to forge ahead

           no matter what befell
             or hid the path,
                  one around whom now

the hurrying crowds move past without a nod or glance.

Surrounded by Vast Silence and Time

Practice
>   doesn't make perfect,
>>   if what one is after

>>   is the shape of thought,
>>>   how it shimmers and stretches
>>>>   and cannot lie still.

>   Better to trace the lightning down the night's wide walls,

losing
>   its motion to the mirroring of memory.
>>   Pointless? I suppose.

>>   Absurd as a daisy
>>>   on the day of one's death?
>>>>   Maybe, maybe not—

yet always there's this self that wants to go

farther,
>   deeper, truer,
>>   a few steps out past

>>   the edge of itself
>>>   to see what, if anything,
>>>>   will hold it aloft.

>   Maybe nothing will, only the sense that one is

losing
>   a voice that might have
>>   mattered once

>>   on a day whose importance
>>>   has likewise fallen away.
>>>>   Something in the way

a prayer begins earnestly, imploringly, only to move

faster
           and faster through the vast silence
                    surrounding it

            until time and its timelessness
                begin to encroach,
                    gathering the words,

touching all sides then letting them fall.

The Bounds of Belief

"There lives the dearest freshness deep down things."
—Gerard Manley Hopkins

Dearest?
      Anymore, such language
            runs the risk

        of being thought extreme,
           grandiose, too certain of itself,
               bold beyond the bounds of belief,

     quaint even—maybe, in some circles, reckless. Any

freshness
      there might have been
           has long since turned stale.

        Doesn't hunger still remain, though,
           this ache to reach up
              out of ourselves,

     the palm at the end of the mind? Isn't there some deeper

deep
      than what our words
           can touch,

        some farther far?
           Where is lightheartedness?
              Where joy, conviction, purpose?

     Where plenitude of spirit, leaping about? Let's get

down
      to the bedrock
           to see if one exists,

        to say a final yes or no.
           In the light of last lights,
              in this bent and broken world,

can there be wings brooding over us or the teaching of all

things
    honest and just, lovely
        and pure? Is uncertainty

     our only certainty? What if questions
     are stall tactics delaying
         answers? What can that mean

for us, charged as we are, seeking what everything means?

Beyond All Odes

Count
  the dove calls of a morning—
    near-silences

    silencing out most other sounds—
    and soon you'll let
      their numbers go

  and sit apprenticed to the endlessness of

all
  that can't be gathered up,
    can't be confirmed

    or made use of, all that
    thinking can't tidy up,
      can't contain,

  can't make fully known. Like a painter, study

things
  —a pear, a blade of grass—
    so that the light

    imprint upon your sense
    of *what can be*
      the inexhaustible subtleties

  of time elapsing as it must and will

but
  not without the brilliance
    of its having been at all.

    The rain (oh let it) could come
    and wash us all away
      beyond all odes and trace

of books, beyond memory, which only amplifies

loss

   of who one was or tried to be:
      a breath upon the morning air,

    unremarkable but attendant;
      a few words balanced against
        their own dissolution;

a low limb trying to lift itself to touch an endless sky.

Emptied of Forethought and What Happens Next

Better
        days are unlikely
                since no other day exists

                but this one,
                        continually returned unto itself,
                                replenished and enlarged,

        cicada-stretched and oak-shadow-woven. May I

learn
        the unreadable text of its passing,
                the irrefutable summons

                inscribed upon my breath,
                        to offer myself up,
                                abeyance and praise,

        emptied of forethought and what happens next.

How
        I breathe, one writer said,
                is important.

                Did he have in mind
                        the vowelless name of God
                                that can't be pronounced,

        only exhaled? Is it dispensation of grace that leads

to
        this need to be still,
                to listen out beyond

                the reach of all words,
                        to hear inside the inside
                                a deeper and deeper call,

21

tender and tinder? May the words from my mouth

kneel,
      bow down, bleed out
              their substance

         till they're wordless and finished,
            husks caught away,
                 moving across grass and stems

in the moment of the moment affirming itself.

Not Reaching to Hold Anything

One
>   willow at the field edge—
>   after weeks away
>
>   I want to wander toward the shape
>   of its meandering
>   pantomime against
>
>   the sky, slow in my own motions, as though

life—
>   the ruminative feel of it—
>   could be experienced bodily,
>
>   felt in the soles of my feet,
>   clutched in the back of my legs,
>   in the tightening tendons,
>
>   in the sway of my arms not reaching to hold anything.

With
>   or without
>   days or years to come,
>
>   I've set my steps toward
>   a grammar, too,
>   I cannot hear or speak,
>
>   wind-whipped and flung about and shadowing along the ground.

Each
>   of the selves I am
>   or think to be
>
>   adds what he can: a word, a prayer,
>   a question whose asking
>   is the falling sound of leaves,

the gape of the hollow, the wing strokes of owls.

Other
            times I only listen
                        to the unlikeliness

                of anything or anyone having been,
                        their *being*
                                sudden and haunting,

fluent and silent, like willow limbs shivered to vanishing.

Fine Distinction

Faith,
  what are you exactly?
      part wish, part desire?

      part hope to believe?
        part asking the next thought
          to empty itself?

  I don't ask not believing, just not knowing.

Is
  my asking a way
      to get closer or farther

      from wandering your wide rooms?
      Yes, I know: *evidence*
        of things not seen,

  yet, being words (thus imprecise), a phrase is only

a
  small light aimed ahead,
      though the walk is long

      —dark and deep, as one man said—
        and perhaps along a ledge
            without assistance.

  Some, content that we infuse all words with

fine
  distinctions we invent
      to make ourselves feel safe,

      seem not to worry
        if an error has been made.
            Is something overlooked?

I doubt this thrust to know what can't be known is my

invention;
for if it were, I'd let it go,
do something mindless—

catch falling leaves, for instance,
and toss them back
into the trees,

over and over till I could feel their shade again.

As Though Each Word Were an Epiphany

for David Till

As

       more and more rain fell,
              it seemed the highest ground

          would not be high enough.
          There'd be no view
               from which to see it all,

       not safely. The farthest news gave little consolation.

I

       thought, as I have often done,
              I want to live

          to understand what meaning is,
             how much eternity
               will fit inside a thought.

       I mean, I've seen it, heard it, in how a teacher

talked

       as though each word
              were an epiphany,

          a gratitude for existence,
             so that across his face
               I glimpsed a passing light

       and his surprise at what had been revealed to him.

I

       always think of creeks, it seems,
              eddies and sandbars,

          rocks I skipped
             touching down once,
               twice, pulsing ahead,

not reaching the other side, the murky depths I

swam
with no one present,
the fear that something

would reach for me
and not let go. Even so,
I couldn't stop myself.

I dove head-first—clutching—deeper through the depths.

For When the Days Seem Absent Any Answers

No

is sometimes the affirmation
a soul most needs,

a mountain brought to its knees
before a valley
stretching miles ahead,

idea so vast the mind cannot contain it. Signs and wonders

lie

everywhere around us,
like the morning I saw

a parking lot puddle
filled with birds (a hundred?)
frolicking and cleansing themselves—

rejoicing, I'm tempted to say, in that way a person

can

discern, without a single doubt,
a message has been given;

for I'll admit that I believe,
have always believed,
such moments seek us out

to show us what's unseen within the life we

live.

So I received it,
spoke *yes* aloud

while sailing over roads
and in and out of neighborhoods,
sang it, really, over and over,

out of tune, I'm sure, though wide awake inside

forever,
    if that's conceivable
        and even if it's not.

      You should have seen me—
        to the ends of my existence
          doing my own cleansed

dance, feeling all around me that cool water's truth.

I Suppose One Day I'll Know for Sure

Where
    pelicans' wings sail the coastline,
        I walk along

        feeling posthumous,
            a soul without
                a single torment,

    mute, wave after wave unfolding eternity at my feet.

Time,
    unhurried, lets
        the meaning of itself

        insist itself, and not without
            extravagance, not without
                the calm *thought* needs

    to pierce immutability, then to ripen.

Lies
    or truths? Or something made
        from both? I suppose

        one day I'll know for certain
            which certainties sank
                to nothingness. I suppose

    my suppositions—so often held, admired—will be

shattered
    by the slightest touch of wind,
        be turned out to dust.

So little will survive to sound
      like prayers in others' thoughts—
            only the whispered words,

how they seemed to know farther than a voice could say them.

Having Weighed the Only Words I Hold

I'm
        that man on the rooftop
                others mistake for a jumper—

           but I am here only to see
              the skyline closer
                   and to get above

the doorposts before the angel passes by.

Nobody
        quite believes me, though,
                for all my words having fallen

           past usefulness.
              I pick them up like stones
                  to glimpse their undersides,

to weigh them in my hands and fling them on.

Who
        is this "we," for instance,
           so often spoken of these days?

           You and I—we're like those farm birds
              leaving fence posts
                  to fly full-bodied

against each other. Still, I believe that we

are
        gifts to one another—
              of that I am sure.

           For such sentimental claims
             I'm often dismissed,
                though I doubt

fiercer words will be found in me.

You

       won't remember
              that boy I was years ago,

          batting rocks across the creek,
            but each arc of flight
               into the brush

was one more forgiveness that reached the other side.

Autobiography

Old
> single-tine combines in the fields back home
> > will not be resurrected.

> > They serve as a reminder
> > > of an era's solitude—
> > > > apostles or prophets

> rusting out their warnings to relinquish

things,
> to be only spirit,
> > like wind through sage grass

> > dancing, twirling, spelling out
> > > a lack of memory,
> > > > a rush of simply being present.

> A new century has come since I was there—the days

are
> blind as ever
> > and lead away into poems

> > whose words I keep revising,
> > > grammar of dust on the tongue
> > > > and seed heads of light,

> the downstream song of a creek-scene already

passed
> out of sight and gone
> > the way of going:

> > a boy holding a stick
> > > tremble-tests the shallows,
> > > > imagines some day

remembering this very gesture slipping

away
        inside a memory
            that will, itself,

           also slip away,
               as though its presence
                  were an absence

briefly glimpsed and touched—then that, too, let go of.

Gladness

for Libby (1953-2008)

Rejoice,
      being intransitive,
            can't perform an action,

        though turning toward joy
           is intrinsic, something inside me
               bent toward praise. Thus,

I begin these words for you, a gladness for our days together,

and,
      while time still believes in me
           and offers me this space,

        I'll try to raise my
           raucous verbs and famished hopes,
               all that's unnamable,

brushed up against my footfalls and shadows. Why

be,
      if all I am is
           all I am and not

        the thoughts of others shared
           and not the consolations found
               and not this lack of knowing

anything entirely, this incessant, broken, immeasurably

exceeding-
      everything-that-can-be-
           said-about-it life?

        Maybe that's why
           I lean toward these words
               to hear them as you might

hear them, words monastic inside their sounds, held-up

glad

        whispers between us.
                            Do you receive them?

            Hear how my voice
                  trembles to stand
                          inside your elegy,

this not knowing how far my not-knowing might reach.

Into Nothing of My Own Making

To
>> follow the current
>>> is to lay aside the paddle,

>>> to sense time's absence
>>>> which, as a young man, I did
>>>>> one morning long before my life

>> came rushing in. I hummed an old song—"What can

make
>> me whole again?
>>> Nothing but the blood of Jesus"—

>>> and stared long into the deep
>>>> surrounding me,
>>>>> my face undone,

>> slipped loose to float among clouds. I think I've always

known
>> the mind wants more
>>> than what is set before it

>>> —flash of purple wing,
>>>> wind-teased leaf about to fall—
>>>>> wants more than what it can imagine,

>> more than what imagination manages to hold.

The
>> creek took me farther and farther
>>> toward the county's core,

>>> into the dawn time of creation,
>>>> into nothing of my own making,
>>>>> into being-where-I-was,

not caring where I was, alive only in the

mystery
    of my presence being
        inscribed upon a moment

    both passing and eternal,
        as the sound of water/
           the water of sound

are time being poured pouring time into being.

Past Argument

Waking
      to the mystery that's all-surrounding—
            isn't that the theme

          poets keep announcing
             down the labyrinthine centuries,
                through book after book,

      word after word, though doubtful anyone is listening?

Before
      a fish leaps lengthwise and shining again,
             I want to be looking with all I am

          at the very spot on the lake,
             a moment past all argument
                stunned into being

      by a faith that has brought it forth.

Morning
      is its own presence allowing my own,
             though even my breath is a trespass

          and my thoughts a trespass
             and my waiting to see *what-is*
                a smudge on the moment

      perfecting itself since time began.

Light
      seeds itself everywhere and grows up out of the ground,
             being the cattails bowing east

and the tadpoles trailing the silt,
        and one day into that same light
                I will vanish—taken-up—

that honeycombed, replete-with-itself, ever-infolding light.

If Design Govern

In
due time perhaps
    we get a glimpse

that all we know
    or can know
        is as a tumbling leaf

the wind snatches elsewhere, wringing forth

a
dust that can't be
    reassembled.

Even our metaphors
    to show the shallowness
      of thinking

can't rise above mundanity, the much diminished

thing
we try to make much of.
    We venture on across

the wide and wider spaces.
    The gaps fill in
      with deeper gaps,

and all our words suggest more words, more words,

so
many they may, in fact,
    fill a universe

itself continually expanding.
    Words, syllables, phonemes,
      each a universe singing

across the space of itself yet strangely spoken by us,

small

as we are and almost nothing, really,
a sliver of width,

a synapse, a slowness,
in the length of all time
barely a breath

yet all that exists that can lift words out of a self.

Blank Page

I
>doubt we'll make it
>>to some aftertime,

>>some grand perspective
>>>looking back on this time
>>>>in the way that, now,

>we think of *yesteryear* and think we

have
>a clearer, truer understanding
>>than we did while walking there.

>>It's just as well
>>>we never fully know
>>>>the folly of our knowing.

>I doubt that we could bear it. The poet's blank page

promises
>everything, then less
>>and less, then finally

>>close to nothing, sometimes
>>>only silence,
>>>>which may, in the end,

>be our true accounting. Whatever the age is coming

to
>we won't be here
>>when it arrives,

>>and all we tried to bring
>>>into being, to say or do,
>>>>will be as breath upon

a windowpane. We've always known this truth, tried to

keep
             from knowing it, tried to
                       stall the quiet afterwards,

                  tried to touch, just out of reach,
                       what keeps us steadily
                               reaching. Sometimes

all we knew to do was keep on going into the empty miles.

What the River Says

That
      I have risen
               yet another morning

          to have this sense
             of being in the world
                 and turned on up the hill

      to look so wide and far in all directions

is
      one more mystery
             of time's unfolding

          I guess I cannot know.
          That I remain
             while others fell away

      is God's great secret, the pleasure of His will.

"What
      is man that you are
             mindful of him,"

          David asked,
            and so did Job,
                our lives compared

      to vapor, to grass, to fig, to lamb, to bread.

I
      have only the same question,
             asked in what I hope

          is a tone of wonder,
             a tone of submission,
                though I know, too, knowing

myself, I hold a part back, my own secret. What I

say

      is what I cannot
                find my way to say,

          though it waits before me,
                this next moment, its stillness,
                    where my foot may find

firm footing or, in due time, slip, and then be led away.

Cold Mind

"Nothing
        matters and what if
                it did," Mellencamp sang,

            and I guess the question
            is ever present,
                the ground upon

    which all the other questions are built—not

that
        we know for sure
            what view of things

            will exist once our time is finished.
            The question as quest,
                as search for truth,

    or ("It depends upon what your definition of *is*

is")
        diversion from truth.
            So much depends

            upon how the construct
            is constructed,
                what lies behind

    what lies behind the lies we tell ourselves are

not
        the lies that others
            tell themselves.

            Cold cold mind,
                "small part of the pantomime,"
                do I hold you,

or you me, and to what are we listening? The

there

    that may or may not
        be there—

       how exactly did we conceive it?
        By what logic?
           In this barren place,

what need brings us to this edgeless edge, beholding?

As Much or as Little

With
　　　another spring upon me,
　　　　　　redbuds out back

　　　　　beginning to catch fire,
　　　　　I feel more *here*
　　　　　　　than ever,

　　　sealed to this life, this little time I have been given.

All
　　　I ask is what
　　　　　　I ask and ask again—

　　　　　for more, for less,
　　　　　　　for as much or as little
　　　　　　　　　as I can bear.

　　　I still believe, as I've said before, that all

creation
　　　knows we walk among it;
　　　　　　it sends, as needed,

　　　　　the sun or shade, wind
　　　　　　or stillness. Even so,
　　　　　　　what role is mine?

　　　Blessed observer before it all? Participant? Shouldn't

I,
　　　too, bend all I am,
　　　　　　reach toward the light,

　　　　　let loose my limbs
　　　　　　　in flung-out ecstasy
　　　　　　　　like forsythia yellowing the wind?

51

I know I'd look silly, but so what. Why is it we'll

sing

      in total abandon
            about a love once lost,

        a heart broken, while all around us,
           answering our ache,
                a plenty abounds?

We note it, if at all, and go on, missing its call to join in.

No Sorrow in Sight

They
    waved me forward
        to get a better look

      when I stepped
        from my dad's truck
           evenings I was taken

    to visit kinfolk or shut-ins. Whiskied-up, one would always

sing
    an old hymn—"I saw the light,
        no more darkness,

      no more night…"—
        until he'd break off weeping
           into himself. Others sang, too,

    cursed, hunkered near stoves. I sat mostly still, wondered how

their
    lives had come to be
        such ramshackle outposts

      far from town, one step
        out of the woods line,
           air stale with cigarette smoke

    and empty cans of Vienna sausage. "All human things of

dearest
    value hang on slender strings,"
        Edmund Waller claimed,

      and decades later I confess
        I think of those old men
           awaiting death,

held now by this thinnest memory. And the words to their

songs
　　　hang in a dusk gone dark,
　　　　　　their houses lost

　　　in the earth now,
　　　　　and I can almost trace
　　　　　　　the quiet my father left with, too, moved

farther and deeper into—and I turn, I follow, I fall in behind.

On Earth

As

    I listen to my "neighbor"
        —the talk show host,

      the pundit on his nightly rant—
      I must admit I struggle
          to discern how generosity of spirit

might call a man to lay aside his selfishness.

It—

    this selfishness, this need
      to bend the facts,

      to gloss the issue,
        to leave out anything that doesn't
          gain advantage—surely we are

made for more. "What a piece of work

is

    a man, how noble in reason,"
      Hamlet said,

      unable, nonetheless, to rise above
        his melancholy, though he would
          "conjure by the rights

of our fellowship" a directness we could use today.

In

    your model prayer, Lord,
      you give us

      such a longing
        to give away our will,
          to close the distance between

our earthly ways and that other, more perfect plan

Heaven
      seems to hide, never lets us
            fully see, though at its core

        this strange idea, *forgiveness*,
          calls us to another life.
              Is that why, noting how I fail,

my grief cannot be overcome and, as you did, I weep?

To Begin

Toward
          some shape of sense emerging,
               some newness,

             this small-self begins,
                self of what next, self of
                    lean into this aching ache *to know*—

how, when, why—not knowing exactly how or when or why.

Some
          claim everything in the universe
               is the only size possible,

             held forth and held together
                by laws I sometimes think
                    I understand and then

as quickly lose. And the fact a person ever exists at all is

overwhelming
      in implications,
               statistically almost impossible,

             yet here I am,
                troubling the still waters
                  of what troubles me,

attempting, yet again, to balance joy against the constant

question
      of when I'll cease to be.
             Small-question, I know,

and really beside the point,
            since simply being here
                        astounds me, though I

make no disturbance, though my questions turn to awe.

Trying to Hear a Prayer

to Wil Mills

I
        come again to find
            these bits of driftwood

           shore-caught and careless,
               some hollow-hearted Sunday evening
                  when I can't remember

what the days were headed toward. I try to

hear
        the prayer you prayed
            beneath a mountain's trees

           as we sat on a bench
               in your life's last month,
                  knowing what we knew

but didn't speak aloud. Once, years earlier, you quoted Yeats'

lake
        isle poem while standing
            in bean rows

           planted near
               a cabin you restored.
                  You sang the poem's

cadence forth, described how words could be like

water,
        cool and clear
            upon the tongue,

           plunging toward the heart's
               deep core, an idea
                  inside which you

shivered, as though the air you breathed were

lapping
            against your whole body,
                        against your cells, water

            to water; and when you closed
                  your eyes, I did, too;
                              and we stood there,

are still standing there, hearing our deepest selves.

The Mind and Soul Growing Wide Withal

"Like,"
　　　　the kids say now,
　　　　　　　　over and over,

　　　　　　or click on Facebook—
　　　　　　　　small affirmations
　　　　　　　　　　　that can't fully explore

　　　the knitted souls of vehicle and tenor, the glimpsed-forth

shining
　　　　of one thing seen
　　　　　　　　through the presence

　　　　　　of another—the way the self
　　　　　　　　more clearly understands
　　　　　　　　　　where it is now

by seeing through the lens of where it came

from.
　　　　One person needs another
　　　　　　　　to get outside

　　　　　　the mind, to conceive
　　　　　　　　what's possible
　　　　　　　　　　even to conceive.

　　　　One tense needs another: is/was or shake/

shook,
　　　　to rattle the insides
　　　　　　　　of what we think

　　　　　　we think, what we
　　　　　　　　know we know,
　　　　　　　　　　what we don't know

we don't know and can't know. Through Laertes'

foil

    we better grasp
           the questions of Hamlet.

      "The inward service
         of the mind and soul
            grows wide withal,"

he says, and we enter ourselves fully, *not* as ourselves.

Who We Are and Might Become

For
        all we've come to know,
                what have we

                left behind? or whom?
                or which words?
                        which part of ourselves

        only the words can bring into existence?

In
        the beginning of these end-of-days,
                how are we

                to speak to one another
                        when it seems the words
                                to enter others' lives

        are disappearing? And how else think of

him—
        the man who sits beside
                a drainage ditch

                outside the mall,
                        belongings brought along,
                                greeting passing cars—

        except as a reminder of what, in truth,

we
        would rather not
                think about, dwell upon, consider.

                Do we not
                        belong to each other,
                                to the words between us

knitting our souls together? The question of how to

live

    is answered by questions
        we do not know to ask,

        bound, as we are,
           by what we imagine
               the words we take into ourselves

    imagine. And what do the words conceive?

And

    whom might we become
        if we could see ourselves

        as worded, spoken into being,
           new creations daily, hourly,
               being born and reborn

    to bring to clearer focus how His spirit still might

move

    upon the formlessness
        of who we are,

        dividing light from darkness,
        providing firmaments
           on which, together,

    we might stand. All creation brings forth seed

and

    fruit, word and deed,
        desire to hear the whisperings

        of wind and rain,
           the smallest voice.
               A man, unbathed, greeting

    passersby—what known or unknown reason does he

have
        for sitting at the entrance,
                a quilt spread out,

        a shopping cart
                held in place
                        by his free hand?

    What words, gathered, explain his joy, looking straight through

our
        windows, into our eyes,
                blessing us, it seems,

                even when we look away. I've heard
                        he's praying, though others
                                claim he speaks

        a nonsense no one understands. He waves. I wave. We are

being
        in the world together,
                as this moment now proclaims;

                and who we are or might become
                        is held forth by a force
                                I can't explain until—I can't explain it—

    I *see* him, and all around us we behold becoming light.

Notes

Sources for "watermark" phrases are as follows:

"In the Biting Wind and Half-Dark": Rainer Rilke's "Archaic Torso of Apollo."
"Giving Time Back to Itself": Psalm 109:4.
"Behind the Story Being Told": U2's "God Part II."
"From There to Here": John 14:27.
"Perfect Silence": Walt Whitman's "When I Heard the Learn'd Astronomer."
"Surrounded by Vast Silence and Time": Elizabeth Bishop's "One Art."
"The Bounds of Belief": Gerard Manley Hopkins' "God's Grandeur."
"Beyond All Odes": Philippians 3:8.
"Emptied of Forethought and What Happens Next": U2's "Mysterious Ways."
"Not Reaching to Hold Anything": U2's "One."
"Fine Distinction": Emily Dickinson's "Faith Is a Fine Invention."
"As Though Each Word Were an Epiphany": William Stafford's "With Kit, Age Seven, at the Beach."
"For When the Days Seem Absent Any Answers": Martin Luther King, Jr.'s "Selma Speech."
"I Suppose One Day I'll Know for Sure": Mary Oliver's "Blossom."
"Having Weighed the Only Words I Hold": Emily Dickinson's "I'm Nobody! Who Are You?"
"Autobiography": 2 Corinthians 5:17.
"Gladness": Matthew 5:12.
"Into Nothing of My Own Making": Ephesians 6:19.
"If Design Govern": Robert Frost's "Design."
"Blank Page": Robert Frost's "Stopping by Woods on a Snowy Evening."
"What the River Says": William Stafford's "Ask Me."
"Cold Mind": Wallace Stevens' "The Snow Man."
"As Much or as Little": Jennie Lee Riddle's "Revelation Song."
"No Sorrow in Sight": Thomas Hardy's "During Wind and Rain."
"On Earth": Matthew 6:10.
"To Begin": T.S. Eliot's "The Love Song of J. Alfred Prufrock."
"Trying to Hear a Prayer": William Butler Yeats' "The Lake Isle of Innisfree."
"The Mind and Soul Growing Wide Withal": Gerard Manley Hopkins' "God's Grandeur."
"Who We Are and Might Become": Acts 17:28.

Acknowledgments

Poems in this manuscript appeared as follows:

Birmingham Poetry Review, "No Sorrow in Sight"; *Grist,* "Surrounded by Vast Silence and Time"; *Nashville Review,* "Behind the Story Being Told"; *Potomac Review,* "As Much or as Little," "To Begin," "What the River Says"; *Southern Review,* "Blank Page," "From There to Here"; *Tupelo Quarterly,* "Having Weighed These Only Words I Hold," "Not Reaching to Hold Anything." "The Mind and Soul Growing Wide Withal" and "The Bounds of Belief" appear in *The World Is Charged: Poetic Engagements with Gerard Manley Hopkins* (Daniel Westover and William Wright, eds, Clemson University Press, 2016).

To friends who have championed these poems through the years, thank you for your encouragement and fellowship: Victoria Clausi, Gary McDowell, Katherine Smith, Chera Hammons, Al Maginnes, Becky Yannayon, and Alice Sanford.

Special gratitude to Michelle Hendrixson Miller, who was present at Buckhead Coffeehouse in 2004 when I first conceived of the idea of a "watermark" phrase, a whispered prayer through which to anchor—and to realign—my own thoughts.

I also celebrate and honor the lives of Claudia Emerson and Wilmer Mills—friends whose belief in this book sustains me still.

About the Author

Jeff Hardin is the author of six previous collections of poetry, most recently *A Clearing Space in the Middle of Being*, *No Other Kind of World*, and *Small Revolution*. His work has been honored with the Nicholas Roerich Prize, the Donald Justice Prize, and the X. J. Kennedy Prize. A chapbook, *Generosity for a Later Generation*, recently appeared from Seven Kitchens Press. He is a professor of English at Columbia State Community College, where he has taught for almost three decades. Visit his website at www.jeffhardin.weebly.com.

CPSIA information can be obtained
at www.ICGtesting.com
Printed in the USA
JSHW040333050422
24597JS00002B/119

9 781948 692809